DEDICATING YOUR HOUSE

DR. ED KING

Parsons Publishing House, LLC
Christiansburg, Virginia

DEDICATING YOUR HOUSE
by Ed King

Parsons Publishing House
Christiansburg, VA 24073 USA
www.ParsonsPublishingHouse.com
Info@ParsonsPublishingHouse.com

This book or parts thereof may not be reproduced in any form, stored in a retrieval system, or transmitted in any form by any means – electronic, mechanical, photocopy, recording or otherwise – without prior written permission of the publisher, except as provided by the United States copyright law.

All Scripture quotations, unless otherwise indicated, are taken from the *Holy Bible, King James Version*, Cambridge, 1769.

Scripture quotations marked (NLT) are taken from the Holy Bible, New Living Translation, copyright 1996. Used by permission of Tyndale House Publishers, Inc., Wheaton, Illinois 60189. All rights reserved.

Scripture quotations marked (CEV) are from the Contemporary English Version Copyright © 1991, 1992, 1995 by American Bible Society, Used by Permission.

Scripture quotations marked (MSG) are taken from THE MESSAGE, copyright © 1993, 1994, 1995, 1996, 2000, 2001, 2002 by Eugene H. Peterson. Used by permission of Nav Press. All rights reserved. Represented by Tyndale House Publishers, Inc.

Scripture quotations marked (ERV) are taken from HOLY BIBLE: EASY-TO-READ VERSION © 2014 by Bible League International. Used by permission."

Copyright © 2017 by Ed King.
All rights reserved.
ISBN-13: 978-1602730861
ISBN-10: 1602730865
Library of Congress Control Number: 2017904832
Printed in the United States of America.
For World-Wide Distribution.

TABLE OF CONTENTS

Introduction		v
1.	Why Dedicate Your House?	1
2.	Distinguishing Characteristics	9
3.	Why Dedication Is Important	15
4.	A Good House	27
5.	Your Home Is An Outpost	39
6.	Spirits Dwell In Houses	45
7.	Dedicating Your House in 8 Steps	49
8.	Dedicating Your House Step 1	51
9.	Dedicating Your House Step 2	55
10.	Dedicating Your House Step 3	65
11.	Dedicating Your House Step 4	71
12.	Dedicating Your House Step 5	75
13.	Dedicating Your House Step 6	77
14.	Dedicating Your House Step 7	85
15.	Dedicating Your House Step 8	89
About the Author		95

DEDICATING YOUR HOUSE

INTRODUCTION

Throughout the many years I have spent in the ministry—preaching, teaching, studying, and listening to thousands of sermons from other pastors and teachers—I have never once come across a message on the subject of dedicating a house to the Lord. In fact, what provoked me to write this book in the first place came from the process of moving into a new home and going through the very same process described in the following chapters. My wife, Nora, and I, always dedicate our homes, and I wanted to share with you the motivations and the methods.

DEDICATING YOUR HOUSE

Dedicating a home of any type to the Lord is essential. You are going to find information in this book that is taken from the Bible that will transform your thinking concerning its significance. After reading this book, you will not want to spend another day living in a house—no matter the size or description—that has not been dedicated to the Lord.

1

WHY DEDICATE YOUR HOUSE?

Throughout the years, my wife Nora and I have moved quite a bit and lived in several different homes. God has been good to us, and we are certainly grateful to Him for all of them. Every time we move into a new home, we make sure that we always dedicate it to the Lord in a very particular way. We always pray over it, bless it, and even receive communion in it.

However, I felt in my spirit that there was still something missing. I never felt deep down that the process was biblically complete or thorough enough. It simply felt like we were neglecting some things. I was confident that we were not doing anything wrong, but simply there was more we could do.

Much Like Dedicating a Child

Actually, dedicating a house is very similar to dedicating a child. If you are anything like us, when your child is born, you immediately ask God to bless them by praying a blessing over them and dedicating their life to the Lord. Then, at some future point, there is a more official time of dedication—a much more public consecration—that extends your faith in a special way.

Your home should garner this same type of consideration. After all, it is the place where you live your life in all of its aspects. We pray over the house even before we move in. After we move, we pray over it once again, giving the home to the Lord, and telling Him how thankful we are to Him.

As my study continued, I had a strong sense that there was more to this subject of home

Why Dedicate Your House?

dedication than I had previously thought. So, at first, simply for my own personal interest, I started making a more in-depth study of the subject. I gathered as much information as I could find—never intending to share it publically with anyone, let alone put it into a book. It was merely an exercise in my personal growth in the Lord.

However, not long into the process, the Lord impressed me to share this message with the body of Christ. So, here we are. If your house is not blessed with the blessings that God wants to heap upon you in abundance—financial blessings, the blessing of a peaceful home, and a harmonious existence among other things—you will be missing out.

Defining "House"

So, let's begin in the book of Acts, chapter 16, where we find some interesting Scripture about the different aspects of the word "house":

DEDICATING YOUR HOUSE

And at midnight Paul and Silas prayed, and sang praises unto God: and the prisoners heard them. And suddenly there was a great earthquake, so that the foundations of the prison were shaken: and immediately all the doors were opened, and every one's bands were loosed. And the keeper of the prison awaking out of his sleep, and seeing the prison doors open, he drew out his sword, and would have killed himself, supposing that the prisoners had been fled. But Paul cried with a loud voice, saying, Do thyself no harm: for we are all here. Then he called for a light, and sprang in, and came trembling, and fell down before Paul and Silas, And brought them out, and said, Sirs, what must I do to be saved? And they said, Believe on the Lord Jesus Christ, and thou shalt be saved, and thy **house**. And they spake unto him the word of the

Lord, and to all that were in his **house**. And he took them the same hour of the night, and washed their stripes; and was baptized, he and all his, straightway (Acts 16:25-33, emphasis added).

What was the author of Acts referring to when he said "house"? Here are four distinct biblical definitions:

1. The House of Israel

The House of Israel is the nation of Israel—the heritage of God that came out of the loins of Abraham. It is the earthly, physical, seed of God.

2. The Individual's Community

As you recall, Jesus could not do any mighty works as long as He was ministering in His hometown. The townspeople did not perceive and honor Him as they should have. Jesus was certainly a prophet, but unfortunately was not viewed by the people as the Son of God, but as an ordinary, common man. They did not recognize who He was or acknowledge the call and anointing on His life.

Jesus made this comment:

> But Jesus, said unto them, A prophet is not without honour, but in his own country, and among his own kin, and in his own **house** (Mark 6:4, emphasis added).

When Jesus made that statement, it differentiated His family from His house; I have to believe He was referring to His house being both His immediate family as well as the community that knew His family. Because of that, we have to conclude that in His reference to "the house," it included those living in and around the area where He grew up. This group was not honoring the call on His life either.

3. An Individual's Household or Family

The House of David comes to mind. Or, forgive me, it could also mean the House of Ed or the House of Steve. You get the picture, I'm sure.

4. The Individual's Physical Residence

It is a residence on a piece of real estate. Brick and mortar, wood, stone, and concrete—building materials that make up the houses where we live. A house that houses the house!

These distinctions need to be made because I want you to understand the subtle nuances. When the Bible says that this particular person's house was saved in Acts 16, it was not talking about a conversion and salvation experience for the brick, mortar, wood, stone, and concrete. Obviously, the reference was clearly directed to the people.

DEDICATING YOUR HOUSE

2

DISTINGUISHING CHARACTERISTICS

The word "house" carries with it some distinguishing characteristics that need to be considered closely. I am focusing on them to illustrate that there are aspects related to the "house" that are not necessarily those we typically think of in the spur of the moment or in significant ways.

The first thought that probably comes to mind when thinking of your household may be your family. However, there are others that might be included, as well. There is the household of faith, as well as the household of believers.

DEDICATING YOUR HOUSE

The Bricks & Mortar

For the purpose of this book, I am talking specifically about dedicating your physical house to the Lord—consecrating the house of bricks, mortar, wood, and stone, where you sleep, eat, and live your daily lives. However, as a result of dedicating the house, it will obviously have an effect on your household. I don't think you can live in an unblessed home and have a blessed life. Where you live and what goes on there is important.

As we saw earlier in the book of Acts:

"And they said, Believe on the Lord Jesus Christ, and thou shalt be saved, and thy **house**" (Acts 16:31, emphasis added).

You and your house will be saved.

> When thou goest out to battle against thine enemies, and seest horses, and chariots, and a people more than thou, be not afraid of

Distinguishing Characteristics

> them: for the Lord thy God is with thee, which brought thee up out of the land of Egypt. And it shall be, when ye are come nigh unto the battle, that the priest shall approach and speak unto the people, And shall say unto them, Hear, O Israel, ye approach this day unto battle against your enemies: let not your hearts faint, fear not, and do not tremble, neither be ye terrified because of them; For the Lord your God is he that goeth with you, to fight for you against your enemies, to save you (Deuteronomy 20:1-4).

The four verses above, deal with men going to war. They talk specifically about soldiers in the army grabbing their weapons and going into battle—standing in the breach, in harm's way.

Let's go on to verse five:

> And the officers shall speak unto the people, saying, What man is there that hath built a new **house**,

and hath not dedicated it? let him go and return to his house, lest he die in the battle, and another man dedicate it (Deuteronomy 20:5, emphasis added).

Dedication is Imperative

As important and even necessary as war can sometimes be—especially if there is an imminent threat to your country—the Bible says that going to war is not as important as dedicating your house. War is certainly an issue of the greatest scale and of the gravest importance, but as significant as it is, the Bible says that in God's perspective, the dedication of the house is even more critical. It would then be appropriate that soldiers be at least temporarily relieved of their duties so they could go through the dedication process.

I don't know if that means anything to you, but it strikes me in a way that I have never once thought about. We seem to be indifferent—even unconcerned—with the prospect of dedicating our homes. "Well maybe I will, or maybe I won't. It's just brick-and-mortar after all. It's no big deal, right?"

Wrong.

God says that it is a very big deal. It was important enough to send a soldier home from the war. We would be smart to start thinking in the same way.

> And what man is he that hath planted a vineyard, and hath not yet eaten of it? **Lest him also go and return unto his house, lest he die in the battle, and another man eat of it** (Deuteronomy 20:6, emphasis added).

God is telling us that this house dedication thing is important. It is vitally important to dedicate your house—sooner rather than later.

DEDICATING YOUR HOUSE

3

WHY DEDICATION IS IMPORTANT

If you are reading this book with your Bible close by, open it up to Psalms, chapter 30. When you get there, look at the short introduction—if there is one—located directly above verse one. In many of our Bibles, it tells us what the chapter is about. My Bible says, "A Psalm and Song at the dedication of the house of David."

This verse is not talking about David's family, nor is it talking about the temple. We know this because God would not let David build the temple because he was a man of war—Solomon had to build it.

David put things away and stored up assets. He prepared the treasury for the building of God's house, but God would not let him build it. Instead, God gave Solomon that opportunity. This is a direct reference to a man of God—called a man after God's own heart—dedicating his house to the Lord. In fact, the entire 30th chapter of the book of Psalms tells of a man of God dedicating his real estate to God. That is serious stuff. At least, God thinks it is.

There is a song at the dedication of the house of David that consists of three primary things: prayer, praise, and giving thanks. We incorporate these things into the eight steps of dedication that we will talk about a little later.

Dedication Comes First

In the church, we use the word "dedicate" quite often as a religious expression. We put a little prefix (re) on it and use it frequently when we talk about rededicating our lives to

Why Dedication is Important

the Lord. An issue pops up, however, when we try to rededicate something that has never been dedicated in the first place. That would be like becoming reacquainted with someone you have never met, or reappointed to a position you have never held. That was a personal problem for me as a young man growing up. I tried to rededicate my life to the Lord before I had even dedicated it to Him. I think the church, as a whole, has the same problem. The important thing is to dedicate that which needs to be dedicated.

Three Important Words for the Church

Three important words have to be considered individually when discussing this thing called the community of God or the church.

1. Christ—Christ the anointed one.

If you are going to think about God, you have to think about Christ. A derivative of the word "Christ" is "Christian" which is a

New Testament word that means "follower of Christ." For the most part, we tend to use this term somewhat loosely. The truth is that many of us say we are Christians, but it may be rather disingenuous. Many times, we do not seem to fit the definition; we fail to follow God and may not be doing the things that He wants us to do.

> "And why call ye me, Lord, Lord and do not the things that I say?" (Luke 6:46).

We must acknowledge that the notion of being a Christian does not fall into many people's preconceived idea of its definition. Because of our intense desire to go to heaven when we die, we call upon the Lord to forgive our sins. We take care of business and put that little matter behind us. We are now forgiven, washed in the blood, and everything's good. We are now Christians on our way to heaven! That may be what you deem Christianity to mean, but it is a long way from the Bible's definition. The all-important question then is: **"Are you doing**

the things that you know God has told you to do?"

2. Christianity

We have a building. We have the words, Christ, and Christian. But there is still another word: Christianity.

The word "Christianity," as far as the world can see, is the interpretation of Christ by the Christians. However, because of an inaccurate depiction of Jesus, the Christ, by some so-called believers, the world has developed a distorted view of Him. Consequently, Christianity as they see it, is not necessarily reality, as we know it.

I'm not discounting the terminology; I am merely pointing out that sometimes we don't understand what we are saying when we say it. For instance, the word "Christianity" is society's interpretation of "the Christ" and not the description that Christ Himself would necessarily use. Although Christ never fails us, sometimes our ingrained definition of Christianity does. I am certainly not saying that it is wrong to use the term, but because "Christianity" is all we have, the interpretation as we use it is sometimes distorted.

3. Dedication

The word "dedicate" is an important word. As stated earlier, we use it many times erroneously as we try to rededicate what has never been dedicated. We are attempting to make resolutions without resolve.

In the context of the church, the phrase "to dedicate" means to set something apart and consecrate it for a sacred purpose. It also means the setting apart of a divine being— God being the obvious choice. We use the word "dedicate" to differentiate things that are more important than others, or used for different reasons. For instance, the microphone that I use when I preach in church on Sunday mornings is dedicated to

Why Dedication is Important

the service of the Lord. I do not use it for anything else.

But dedication can take on other forms as well. Following that same line of thought, the lead singer of a famous rock band may be using the exact brand and model of microphone that I use, but has dedicated it to his lead vocals and nothing else. In both instances, they have been appropriated for specific, essential purposes.

I'm sure there is an electrical outlet in your home that has been installed in a particular place, for a specific use—like the outlet installed in your laundry room that's dedicated expressly for an electric clothes dryer. Due to the dryer's sizeable power consumption, no other appliance can share its circuit. It is **dedicated** for a single purpose.

The word "dedicate" in the Bible actually means "narrow." In other words, it is focused

DEDICATING YOUR HOUSE

and has been appointed for an exclusive use. It is dedicated for a singular purpose.

A Narrow Purpose

The word "narrow" is partially defined as 1) being limited in range or scope, or 2) careful, thorough, or minute, as a scrutiny, search, or inquiry.[1] Another definition is: to devote to a sacred purpose or use by a solemn act or a religious ceremony.

A few years ago, our church built a beautiful, new sanctuary, and we dedicated it to the Lord. We prayed over the new building on our first Sunday in it, and we had a formal dedication ceremony later on that year.

That is exactly what I told my wife, Nora, concerning our house. I told her that I was thankful for it, and we would certainly pray over it and bless it, but I wanted to give more thought to the overall process before we dedicated it. I didn't want to go through the process nonchalantly. I wanted to do it appropriately and with the seriousness that I believe it required. We ended up dedicating it a few weeks later.

Acting on Our Understanding

With this understanding, God wants us to set apart, consecrate, dedicate, and devote our homes, houses, and dwellings unto Him. He wants your house dedicated to Him.

The Bible tells us in Proverbs:

"Through wisdom is an house builded; and by understanding it is established:" (Proverbs 24:3).

You should build your house using wisdom and understanding. That means so much more than the physical act of pouring concrete, constructing walls, and installing the plumbing. It can and does mean that, but it also means building the personal things that go on in the house—relationships, activities, and many other things that create a life.

DEDICATING YOUR HOUSE

"A woman's family is held together by her wisdom, but it can be destroyed by her foolishness" (Proverbs 14:1, CEV).

The Bible specifically instructs women with regard to their house. It says that there are women who can tear down their house by their actions. From this verse, we can see it is possible to either build or tear down your house. We'll look at a couple more translations of this verse:

> A wise woman makes her home what it should be, but the home of a foolish woman is destroyed by her own actions (Proverbs 14:1, ERV).

"A wise woman builds her home, but a foolish woman tears it down with her own hands" (Proverbs 14:1, NLT).

There is a difference between building a house and establishing it. But it takes wisdom and understanding to move us into the future of what that house is supposed to mean to our family corporately and to us

Why Dedication is Important

individually. We would do well to spend time before God figuring out just what place your home holds in your family's life.

[1] *Dictionary.com website*

DEDICATING YOUR HOUSE

4

A GOOD HOUSE

> Beware that thou forget not the Lord thy God, in not keeping his commandments, and his judgments, and his statutes, which I command thee this day: Lest when thou hast eaten and art full, and hast built goodly houses, and dwelt therein; (Deuteronomy 8:11-12).

God warns us not to forget Him when we come into a good house and dwell in it. God wants us in a nice home.

Some of you might be thinking that because we are just here on the earth temporarily and on our way to heaven, that it really doesn't matter if we live in a nice home or something more similar to a rat hole. Well, I think it does matter. I think a good home is a testament to who you are—a testimony to your life and a part of your legacy.

The Right Fit

When we started looking for a new home, it was not a quick process. In fact, it took about three years to complete. We would go look at a place and envision living there, but we would eventually conclude that it was not the right fit for us. One after another, all the houses we looked at were very nice, but they just did not feel right.

Please don't take this the wrong way, but as we were looking at one particular house, I told Nora that I didn't feel like the house was good enough for us. The house was certainly nice enough, but there were things about it that did not measure up to our standards. Well, you may say that's just pride, and that I should not say things like that. I disagree; I absolutely should say those things and so should you. There are certain things that are simply not good enough for you. God even said that about Adam.

It Was Good

If you remember, God went through the process of creation saying how good everything was. This isn't an exhaustive list, but you'll get the point ...

- "Let there be light!" That was good.
- He created the division of the earth and the sea; that was good.
- He created the sun, moon, and the stars that separated the light from the darkness; that was good, too.
- God created the fish of the sea, the fowls of the air, and the animals of the earth; He also created the trees, shrubs, and plants; all these were good, as well.

When God directed His attention to Adam, however, He saw that Adam was not nearly good enough by himself. Adam needed something more. So, God built him a woman because he did not yet have enough. He had the entire creation in front of him, but it wasn't good enough.

Then God Built Eve

The woman was the highest form of God's creation. He needed to put women here to spruce things up. No intelligent person would argue with that. The crown jewel of God's creation was the woman.

Blessings and Curses

Among many other blessings that God wants you to have, as we learned earlier, is a good house, and He wants you to enjoy living in it. Let's look at the 28th chapter of Deuteronomy where it talks about the blessings that come upon man through his covenant with God:

> And it shall come to pass, if thou shalt hearken diligently unto the voice of the Lord thy God, to observe and to do all his

commandments which I command thee this day, that the Lord thy God will set thee on high above all nations of the earth: And all these blessings shall come on thee, and overtake thee, if thou shalt hearken unto the voice of the Lord thy God. Blessed shalt thou be in the city, and blessed shalt thou be in the field. Blessed shall be the fruit of thy body, and the fruit of thy ground, and the fruit of thy cattle, the increase of thy kine, and the flocks of thy sheep. Blessed shall be thy basket and thy store. Blessed shalt thou be when thou comest in, and blessed shalt thou be when thou goest out. The Lord shall cause thine enemies that rise up against thee to be smitten before thy face: they shall come out against thee one way, and flee before thee seven ways. The Lord shall command the blessing upon thee in thy storehouses, and in all that thou settest thine hand unto; and he shall bless thee in the land which the Lord thy God giveth thee. The Lord shall establish thee an holy people unto himself, as he hath sworn unto thee, if thou shalt keep the commandments of the Lord thy God, and walk in his ways. And all people of the earth shall see that thou art called by the name of the Lord; and they shall be afraid of thee. And the Lord shall make thee plenteous in goods, in the fruit of thy body, and in the fruit of thy cattle, and in the fruit of thy ground, in the land which the Lord sware unto thy fathers to give thee. The Lord shall open unto thee his good treasure, the heaven to give the rain unto thy land in his season, and to bless all the work of thine hand: and thou shalt lend unto many nations, and thou shalt not borrow. And the Lord shall make thee the head, and not the tail; and thou shalt be above only, and thou shalt not be beneath; if that thou hearken unto the commandments of the Lord thy God, which I command thee this day, to observe and to do them: And thou shalt not go aside from any of the words which I command thee this day, to the right hand, or to the left, to go after other gods to serve them (Deuteronomy 28:1-14).

Blessing after blessing will be yours if you obey the voice of the Lord. But what will happen if you don't?

The curses will come.

> But it shall come to pass, if thou wilt not hearken unto the voice of the Lord thy God, to observe to do all his commandments and his statutes which I command thee this day; that all these curses shall come upon thee, and overtake thee: Cursed shalt thou be in the city, and Cursed shall be thy basket and thy store. Cursed shall be the fruit of thy body, and the fruit of thy land, the increase of thy kine, and the flocks of thy sheep. Cursed shalt thou be when thou comest in, and cursed shalt thou be when thou goest out. The Lord shall send upon thee cursing, vexation, and rebuke, in all that thou settest thine hand

unto for to do, until thou be destroyed, and until thou perish quickly; because of the wickedness of thy doings, whereby thou hast forsaken me. The Lord shall make the pestilence cleave unto thee, until he have consumed thee from off the land, whither thou goest to possess it. The Lord shall smite thee with a consumption, and with a fever, and with an inflammation, and with an extreme burning, and with the sword, and with blasting, and with mildew; and they shall pursue thee until thou perish. And thy heaven that is over thy head shall be brass, and the earth that is under thee shall be iron. The Lord shall make the rain of thy land powder and dust: from heaven shall it come down upon thee, until thou be destroyed. The Lord shall cause thee to be smitten before thine enemies: thou shalt go out one way against them, and flee seven ways before them: and shalt be removed into all the kingdoms of the earth. And thy carcase shall be meat unto

A Good House

all fowls of the air, and unto the beasts of the earth, and no man shall fray them away. The Lord will smite thee with the botch of Egypt, and with the emerods, and with the scab, and with the itch, whereof thou canst not be healed. The Lord shall smite thee with madness, and blindness, and astonishment of heart: And thou shalt grope at noonday, as the blind gropeth in darkness, and thou shalt not prosper in thy ways: and thou shalt be only oppressed and spoiled evermore, and no man shall save thee. Thou shalt betroth a wife, and another man shall lie with her: **thou shalt build an house, and thou shalt not dwell therein**: thou shalt plant a vineyard, and shalt not gather the grapes thereof (Deuteronomy 28:15-30, emphasis added).

It's a Curse Not to Enjoy Your House

God says that it is wrong for you to be unable to enjoy your house. To never be able

DEDICATING YOUR HOUSE

to live in a house you build is a curse. How frustrating that would be! We see one of the curses listed in Deuteronomy 23:30:

> Thou shalt betroth a wife, and another man shall lie with her: thou shalt build an house, and thou shalt not dwell therein: thou shalt plant a vineyard, and shalt not gather the grapes thereof.

The Living Bible says it this way:

> Someone else will marry your fiancée; someone else will live in the house you build; someone else will eat the fruit of the vineyard you plant (Deuteronomy 28:30).

You Have to Live in Your House

"Living in your house" means much more than just existing in it. There is more to it than just having a place to get out of the rain. "Living" in my house means taking off my shoes, propping my feet up on the couch or coffee table and getting comfortable. I'm going to set the thermostat on my HVAC system wherever I want it—making it as cool in the summer and as warm in the winter as my little heart desires. I am going to turn the ceiling fans on high if I want to and then relax my way. I am living my life in this thing. I am not here to serve the house; the house is here to serve me.

Too Perfect?

When Nora and I built our first home some years ago, it was easy to see that she was incredibly gifted with an ability to decorate. She puts things together beautifully that most other people can't imagine. She loves to do the things that turn a house into a home. She has a "touch."

Like everything in her life, our first home was spotless. It was perfect. It looked very nice, especially for us at that time in our lives. It was a beautiful home, but I was having a hard time living there. I was afraid to touch anything. If I only had a dollar for every time I heard, "Don't eat on the couch!" or "Pick up your shoes!" Lord help me if I ever put my feet on the coffee table! Do you understand? We were serving the house. It wasn't long until Nora and I had to have a grown-up-person talk—not an argument, but a conversation.

I told her that we had to live our lives in that house. I mentioned that we were not there to serve the house; it was there to serve us. So, we had the talk, and we met each other in the middle. The result was that she gave a little, and I gave a little; life was good.

God will give you many things if you keep your perspective in line with His direction. God wants you to have nice things, but he doesn't want those nice things to have you.

5

YOUR HOME IS AN OUTPOST

"And daily in the temple, and in every house, they ceased not to teach and preach Jesus Christ" (Acts 5:42).

God says that your house is supposed to be an outpost for teaching and preaching Jesus Christ. If it is not, the will of God is not being followed as it should. Your house is not dedicated appropriately to its purpose.

You might think that your home is not nice enough to receive guests. Please do not put yourself down by falling into that trap. Your home is just fine. After all, the people who live next door to you know what the neighborhood is like. Never use that as an excuse. Your home is your castle. Just make sure your castle doesn't have a year's worth of pizza boxes and soda cans stacked up around the television! Clean it up, and everything will be okay.

Your house is a mission outpost to your community. You might say, "But we're not supposed to have church services here." You may honestly believe that, but it just isn't true. You see, I started the church that I now pastor in the living room of a friend's home, and we've been a vibrant church going strong for over 35 years. That living room helped this church to have a strong foundation.

You should understand that God's call on your life may not be the same as His call on mine, but you should still use your home for the expansion and development of God's Kingdom. You may never have a formal church, but everyone can have a form of a church right where you live.

Your Home is an Outpost

Your mission is on your block, and your house is a witness. Take care of it. Mow the waist-high grass for crying out loud! Clean it up, and pick up the trash that people have been throwing in your yard for months. Paint it, and plant some flowers. Make it a testimony to the glory of the Lord.

Take responsibility for your "little piece of heaven" and you will see something amazing begin to happen. You will notice that your neighbors will start having more pride in their property and will begin to maintain it on an ongoing basis. Act responsibly regarding your property, and your neighbors will start to act the same way, too.

Even the great apostle Paul had meetings from house to house.

> And how I kept back nothing that was profitable unto you, but have shewed you, and have taught you publicly, and from house to house (Acts 20:20).

Visiting Other Houses

> "And when ye come into an house, salute it" (Matthew 10:12).

Matthew is talking about a physical house. When you come into the house, salute it. The word "salute" means to greet or speak a greeting over it.

> And if the house be worthy, let your peace come upon it: but if it be not worthy, let your peace return to you (Matthew 10:13).

Remember, not every house is worthy or good enough for you. If the house is not worthy, then let your peace return to you. In other words, you have the power to speak a physical blessing of peace over a house and expect that blessing to abide and remain on it.

Don't Let Your House Be Disqualified

There are conditions in a house, however, which disqualify it for the service of the

Lord. For example, you cannot take a house full of pornography and dedicate it to the Lord. It would not be worthy of the blessing. Other things would exclude it as well; that's just one example.

God wants a house that is worthy, and He says that you have the power to speak a blessing over it. If it is, in fact, worthy, the blessing—the peace of God—will rest on it, and will be there to stay. God wants peace in your house.

Do you see why it is important to dedicate your home? God does not want you to have a house full of strife and turmoil.

DEDICATING YOUR HOUSE

6

SPIRITS DWELL IN HOUSES

I believe that spirits dwell in houses. I am not talking about some sort of biblical poltergeist, but I'm convinced that spirits of all types live in people's homes. It largely depends on what is happening there currently or what has occurred there in the past.

The Bible tells us there are evil territorial spirits. They will reside in our homes if precautions are not taken. Some of these spirits are stronger than others, and they may have been on that property long before the house was even built. On the other hand, someone may have summoned them there after the house was occupied. You won't necessarily know what brought the spirits to that house. With that said, God wants you to live in a house of peace and not a home of constant torment.

When Nora and I first went into the ministry, we bought a house merely out of convenience. We didn't buy it because we really liked it; we just felt like it was wiser to buy one than pay rent. We didn't like it a great deal, but we thought it was okay because we didn't intend to stay there for long.

Strange Things Began to Happen

But something strange started happening to me as it concerned that house. Every time I would get within two blocks of it, I started getting angry. I wasn't angry at the house necessarily; I would just get upset in general. I didn't even know what I was getting mad at. I could have had a great day where everything went perfectly, but as I got within two blocks of that house, I started

Spirits Dwell in Houses

getting upset. I wasn't mad at anything or anyone in particular, I would just get all bent out of shape for no apparent reason.

I would go into that house and almost immediately pitch a fit about something. It defied logic. It was then that I learned a house can absolutely be strife infested.

We came to discover that the people who we bought the house from had recently gone through a nasty divorce. The house had a spirit of strife on it, and we were never able to get rid of it. That house had the same spirit on it when we left.

That house was not worthy of us. Do you see what I mean? We consistently spoke words of peace over that house, but that peace would not stay on it. It would fly back in our faces. That is the only house we ever had like that, and I do not ever want another one like it.

though the house belongs to them. Many have been amazed at the great change that has come over their home and family after dedicating their house to the Lord.

DEDICATING YOUR HOUSE

7

DEDICATING YOUR HOUSE IN 8 STEPS

This book is unique. Although the dedication of houses to the Lord is certainly not a new concept, I have never heard of anyone laying out the process in such a systematic way. The information in this book will truly bless you and will hopefully make life in your home much more satisfying.

So what's the process we have to go through in order to dedicate our homes? To properly dedicate your house, eight individual procedures or actions will need to be performed.

DEDICATING YOUR HOUSE

8

DEDICATING YOUR HOUSE
STEP ONE

Set Your House Apart Verbally Before God

Joshua said, "...but as for me and my house, we will serve the Lord." If you are going to dedicate your house to the Lord, you must open your mouth and set it apart before Him verbally. No one else can do it for you. Your pastor could certainly come over and assist you in the process, but he cannot do for you what you must do for yourself. If your house needs to be dedicated to the Lord, you are personally going to have to dedicate it.

DEDICATING YOUR HOUSE

Joshua made this declaration concerning his house. He said:

> And if it seem evil unto you to serve the Lord, choose you this day whom ye will serve; whether the gods which your fathers served that were on the other side of the flood, or the gods of the Amorites, in whose land ye dwell: but as for me and my house, we will serve the Lord (Joshua 24:15).

We know that Joshua was referring to the members of his family that lived in the house with him. However, I am also confident that the physical house is a direct reflection of the family that resides within it. In fact, I absolutely do not believe that the house can exist without being a reflection of its inhabitants. That being said, neither do I believe that the brick and mortar of the house can be excluded.

One of the most significant declarations of my life is included in the passage above: "As for me and my house, we will serve the

Dedicating Your House—Step One

Lord." In fact, it is important enough that I have those words prominently engraved on the most prominent place of entry to our home—the front door. Before anyone even rings the doorbell, they will see those words prominently displayed before them on the doorknocker. When reading it, they are made aware of the priorities that guide our lives—in some cases, even before they meet us. As for me, and my house, we will serve the Lord.

You may think that the doorknocker idea is trivial, but it is extremely important to me. Not only is it a declaration to anyone stepping up on my front porch, but the devil also needs to know the significance of that short little sentence. I want to make sure he knows that he doesn't belong in my house

DEDICATING YOUR HOUSE

9

DEDICATING YOUR HOUSE
STEP TWO

Cleanse Your House from All Uncleanness

> And the Lord spake unto Moses and unto Aaron, saying, When ye be come into the land of Canaan, which I give to you for a possession, and I put the plague of leprosy in a house of the land of your possession (Leviticus 14:33-34).

It was not the Lord who put leprosy there. It was already there; it existed there.

> And he that owneth the house shall come and tell the priest, saying, It

> seemeth to me there is as it were a plague in the house: (Leviticus 14:35).

Leprosy in the Old Testament is a type of sin. The Bible says that there can be sin abiding in the house that is so saturated that the house has become unworthy and unable to be cleansed. There may have been activities that happened in that house that put it outside the possibility of complete cleansing. You may not be able to cleanse all of it.

> Then the priest shall command that they empty the house, before the priest go into it to see the plague, that all that is in the house be not made unclean: and afterward the priest shall go in to see the house: (Leviticus 14:36).

Rid Your Home of Demonic Influences

What does that mean? Eliminate any items from your home that do not need to be there. Toss those Buddha statues into the trash. Stop your subscription to *Astrology*

Dedicating Your House—Step Two

Believers Magazine and throw the remaining issues away. Who cares if you are a Virgo, Scorpio, or a Capricorn? Get that nonsense out of your house. It is nothing but witchcraft. Remember King Saul?. He lost his kingdom for consulting a witch.

> The Philistines set up their camp at Shunem, and Saul gathered all the army of Israel and camped at Gilboa. When Saul saw the vast Philistine army, he became frantic with fear. He asked the Lord what he should do, but the Lord refused to answer him, either by dreams or by sacred lots or by the prophets. Saul then said to his advisers, "Find a woman who is a medium, so I can go and ask her what to do." His advisers replied, "There is a medium at Endor." So Saul disguised himself by wearing ordinary clothing instead of his royal robes. Then he went to the woman's home at night, accompanied by two of his men (1 Samuel 28:4-8, NLT).

Saul was in deep trouble because his enemy, the Philistines, were at war with him. He was fearful and felt like God had forgotten him; he needed an answer to know what he should do.

So he called on a witch.

Are you going to do the same thing? Are you going to consult the astrologers and the psychics when you know very well that God forbids it? I would much rather have God on my side than against me, wouldn't you?

A House Not Worthy

You may have found yourself with a house that is not worthy of dedication because you have not done one thing to clean it. You might say, "I know that some people think that shrunken head hanging on the wall in my den is pagan, but it's just a souvenir that a medicine man in Africa gave me. I don't even believe in it." Okay, if you don't believe in it, get it out of there. Just use some common sense.

Look at a couple of verses in the book of Leviticus:

> Then the priest shall come and look, and, behold, if the plague be spread in the house, it is a fretting leprosy in the house; it is unclean (Leviticus 14:44).

> And if the priest shall come in, and look upon it, and, behold, the plague hath not spread in the house, after the house was plaistered: then the priest shall pronounce the house clean, because the plague is healed. And he shall take to cleanse the house two birds, and cedar wood, and scarlet, and hyssop: And he shall kill the one of the birds in an earthen vessel over running water: And he shall take the cedar wood, and the hyssop, and the scarlet, and the living bird, and dip them in the blood of the slain bird, and in the running water, and sprinkle the house seven times: (Leviticus 14:48-51).

Give an Offering

An offering can go a long way to help cleanse your house. I want you to notice something in verse 52. Today, we would give a different type of offering, but in this verse, there was an offering given of a bird, cedar wood, hyssop, and scarlet.

> And he shall cleanse the house with the blood of the bird, and with the running water, and with the living bird, and with the cedar wood, and with the hyssop, and with the scarlet (Leviticus 14:52).

Plead the Blood

The priest cleansed the house with the blood of the bird. We as Christians need to plead the blood of Jesus over our dwellings as well. After all, it was the blood of Jesus Christ that cleansed us.

You will cleanse your house with the blood of Christ. You don't cleanse it with the blood

Dedicating Your House—Step Two

of an animal sacrifice any longer; all that is over. The blood of Christ and the testimony of God cleanse the house. Apply it to your house today.

I think that it's a good idea when you take communion in your house to take some of that juice or wine and symbolically put it above the doorpost. It's not because the liquid has any power in and of itself, but because of what it symbolizes. The blood cleanses it!

We find this example in the Passover. The people took the blood of a lamb, and they put it over the lintel—the supporting beam over a door or window—and on the doorpost of their house. When the death angel came by, the Bible says that it passed over the houses with the blood on the doorposts because it could not penetrate it. The destroyer could not enter that house because of the bloodline.

Let's look in Exodus 12, starting with verse 21.

DEDICATING YOUR HOUSE

> Then Moses called for all the elders of Israel, and said unto them, Draw out and take you a lamb according to your families, and kill the passover. And ye shall take a bunch of hyssop, and dip it in the blood that is in the bason, and strike the lintel and the two side posts with the blood that is in the bason; and none of you shall go out at the door of his house until the morning. For the Lord will pass through to smite the Egyptians; and when he seeth the blood upon the lintel, and on the two side posts, the Lord will pass over the door, and will not suffer the destroyer to come in unto your houses to smite you (Exodus 12:21-23).

Are you beginning to see the importance of dedicating your property? The Bible is full of references to it. Dedicate your house. Apply the blood to it.

> And they shall take of the blood, and strike it on the two side posts

Dedicating Your House—Step Two

> and on the upper door post of the houses, wherein they shall eat it (Exodus 12:7).

Put the blood on the doorpost. It saved the people of Israel, and it can save you."

> And the blood shall be to you for a token upon the houses where ye are: and when I see the blood, I will pass over you, and the plague shall not be upon you to destroy you, when I smite the land of Egypt (Exodus 12:13).

Wherever the Death Angel saw the blood on the doorpost, it passed over that particular house and the plague did not enter it. We, as Christians, need to plead the blood over our dwellings, too.

> For the Lord will pass through to smite the Egyptians; and when he seeth the blood upon the lintel, and on the two side posts, the Lord will

DEDICATING YOUR HOUSE

pass over the door, and will not suffer the destroyer to come in unto your houses to smite you (Exodus 12:23).

10

DEDICATING YOUR HOUSE
STEP THREE

Walk Your Property Lines

"Walk my property lines? That sounds like a bit much. Why should I do that?" Okay, look at what the Bible says, and notice how it is worded.

> Therefore shall ye lay up these my words in your heart and in your soul, and bind them for a sign upon your hand, that they may be as frontlets between your eyes. And ye shall teach them your children, speaking of them when thou sittest in thine house, and **when thou walkest by the way,** when thou liest

DEDICATING YOUR HOUSE

down, and when thou risest up (Deuteronomy 11:18-19, emphasis added).

If you have kids, teach them in your house. However, you can only do that if you have a worthy house; you have to have a good one.

"And thou shalt write them upon the door posts of thine **house**, and upon thy gates:" (Deuteronomy 11:20, emphasis added).

Put the Word on the doorpost and put Scriptures around the house. Do you realize that only those things that you have knowledge of can be received from the Lord? You can't receive from God what you don't know anything about. The Bible says it this way:

> Bless the Lord, O my soul, and **forget not all his benefits**: Who forgiveth all thine iniquities; who healeth all thy diseases; Who redeemeth thy life from destruction; who crowneth thee with lovingkindness and tender

Dedicating Your House—Step Three

> mercies; Who satisfieth thy mouth with good things; so that thy youth is renewed like the eagle's (Psalm 103:2-5, emphasis added).

If you can't remember all of the many benefits that you have as a result of your relationship with God, you won't have access to them. It would be a great idea to place touchstones—or reminders—around you as prompts of what God has done in your life. If you have found yourself without a job, and God miraculously gave you a great one, frame a copy of the date it happened, and put it in a prominent place. If he miraculously healed you, do the same thing. If you don't, you'll soon forget them, and the positive influence they would have had in your life will be gone.

Notice that this verse is talking about your house:

> That your days may be multiplied, and the days of your children, in the land which the Lord sware unto

> your fathers to give them, as the days of heaven upon the earth (Deuteronomy 11:21).

You can make your house a place of heaven on the earth. That is not living in torment, is it? A little heaven on earth. You see, a worthy house is a house full of heaven right here on earth.

> For if ye shall diligently keep all these commandments which I command you, to do them, to love the Lord your God, to walk in all his ways, and to cleave unto; Then will the Lord drive out all these nations from before you, and ye shall possess greater nations and mightier than yourselves. Every place whereon the soles of your feet shall tread shall be yours: from the wilderness and Lebanon, from the river, the river Euphrates, even unto the uttermost sea shall your coast be (Deuteronomy 11:22-24).

These verses are talking about your house. An enemy that comes against your house can be put under foot by taking your feet and placing them one in front of the other, walking your property line and taking ownership of it in the spirit. Physically tread on your real estate—all of it if possible. I am not talking about mowing it either. I'm talking about walking it on purpose, in faith, believing that it is going to do some good. Possess it! Dedicate it to God.

DEDICATING YOUR HOUSE

11

DEDICATING YOUR HOUSE
STEP FOUR

Speak Peace to the House

"And my people shall dwell in a peaceable habitation, and in sure dwellings, and in quiet resting places;" (Isaiah 32:18).

Write that verse down in large letters—or have it professionally printed and framed—and hang it on a prominent wall in your house. That is a definition of what your house should be. Put it on a doorpost.

> And into whatsoever house ye enter, first say, Peace be to this house. And if the son of peace be

> there, your peace shall rest upon it: if not, it shall turn to you again. And in the same house remain, eating and drinking such things as they give: for the labourer is worthy of his hire. Go not from house to house (Luke 10:5-7).

If You Can't Clean It, Don't Live In It!

The apostle Luke, by the inspiration of God, said to not remain in a house where you can't get the peace of God to stay on it. "I think we can cleanse any house," you may say. I'm confident you'll find that some of them can be cleansed, but some of them you cannot.

God said not to stay in a house that you cannot clean up. You are not aware of what went on in there. You have absolutely no idea what happened inside those walls before those walls were yours. You are taking too much of a chance.

I have preached in various places around the world, and I have known in my spirit that

Dedicating Your House—Step Four

there was no way to have an anointed church service in that building. There was simply too much demonic influence stored up there.

You might say, "Just pray and bind the devil. Case closed. Problem solved." Yes, I know, but I don't want to do that every single day of my life. Why would I want to go into my house every day and have to bind the devil before I can sit down? That's not going to happen. I am not going to be a servant to that when I can live somewhere else.

DEDICATING YOUR HOUSE

12

DEDICATING YOUR HOUSE
STEP FIVE

Invite God's Presence Through Prayer

Here is a very good verse you can use in the process of dedicating your house:

> Yet have thou respect unto the prayer of thy servant, and to his supplication, O Lord my God, to hearken unto the cry and to the prayer, which thy servant prayeth before thee to day: **That thine eyes may be open toward this house night and day,** even toward the place of which thou hast said, My name shall be there: **that thou**

DEDICATING YOUR HOUSE

mayest hearken unto the prayer which thy servant shall make toward this place (1 Kings 8:28-29, emphasis added).

This is another verse to put in a visible place in your home. By doing this, you are saying a great deal to God. You are saying, "God, bring Your presence on this house and don't turn Your eyes away from it! Bring Your presence into this house and look after it night and day."

When tornadoes occur, they will not come to my house! They will just have to find another path and go around my real estate. They are not allowed there. You may think this is crazy, but it isn't crazy if it works! Invite God's presence into your house through prayer.

13

DEDICATING YOUR HOUSE
STEP SIX

Speak Blessings Over Your House and Your Property

There are gazillions of various verses found in the Bible that can be easily used to speak blessings over your house. Even so, for time's sake, we'll look at just a few. First, let's look at a couple of verses from the book of Deuteronomy,

> And it shall be, when the Lord thy God shall have brought thee into the land which he sware unto thy fathers, to Abraham, to Isaac, and to Jacob, to give thee great and goodly

> cities, which thou buildedst not, And houses full of all good things, which thou filledst not, and wells digged, which thou diggedst not, vineyards and olive trees, which thou plantedst not (Deuteronomy 6:10-11).

Let's look at that same verse with a more contemporary feel,

> The Lord your God made a promise to your ancestors, Abraham, Isaac, and Jacob. He promised to give you this land, and he will give it to you. He will give you great and rich cities that you did not build. He will give you houses full of good things that you did not put there. He will give you wells that you did not dig. He will give you vineyards and olive trees that you did not plant, and you will have plenty to eat (Deuteronomy 6:10-11, ERV).

Dedicating Your House—Step Six

Deuteronomy 6:11 in the New Living Translation says that your house will be greatly supplied.

> "The houses will be richly stocked with goods you did not produce..."
> (Deuteronomy 6: 11, NLT).

The idea here is to **speak** the blessing. Go out on your front lawn and tell your house to fill up with all kinds of good things. Say to your house, "Fill up, house! I'm tired of having these empty rooms. Fill up, you hear me! Fill up with the best things, not the cheap stuff."

You Want the Best in Your House

Don't ever be satisfied with orange crates for furniture. Not anymore. You are now through with filling up your house with furniture you found on the side of the road! Every time you see a furniture truck driving down the street, go out there and look; it's probably coming to your house. But don't take it upon yourself and fill your house up by using your credit card or the store's finance plan. There is a much better way. Even if it takes a little longer, the wait will certainly be worth it.

Another Great Verse for Your House

> Now therefore let it please thee to bless the house of thy servant, that it may be before thee for ever: for thou blessest, O Lord, and it shall be blessed for ever (1 Chronicles 17:27).

The same verse in the New Living Translation says this,

> And now, it has pleased you to bless the house of your servant, so that it will continue forever before you. For when you grant a blessing, O Lord, it is an eternal blessing!" (1 Chronicles 17:27, NLT).

Dedicating Your House—Step Six

Wealth & Riches

Let's look at Psalms, chapter 112:

> Praise ye the Lord. Blessed is the man that feareth the Lord, that delighteth greatly in his commandments. His seed shall be mighty upon earth: the generation of the upright shall be blessed. Wealth and riches shall be in his house: and his righteousness endureth for ever (Psalms 112:1-3).

Wealth and riches are in the house! Your covenant promises that very thing. However, if you find yourself in an unworthy house, you may be unable to obtain it. God won't bring wealth and riches to anything or anyone deemed unworthy.

This may be the first time you have ever heard anything like this and may be having a hard time digesting it. Well, hang in there; it will be worth it. This book can absolutely revolutionize your life and totally change it forever.

Some of you are haunted with where you live because you are living in houses not worthy of you. Here's what Proverbs 3:33 says:

> " The curse of the Lord is in the house of the wicked: but he blesseth the habitation of the just" (KJV).

> "The Lord curses the house of the wicked, but he blesses the home of the upright." (NLT)

Proverbs 15:6 talks about meeting your obligations, so that your habitations or houses are blessed by the Lord. You can see the depth of this verse by reading it in a couple of different translations.

> "In the house of the righteous is much treasure: but in the revenues of the wicked is trouble"(KJV).

Dedicating Your House—Step Six

"The lives of God-loyal people flourish; a misspent life is soon bankrupt" (MSG).

The blessing in your house is the cradle of all of your prosperity. Your house is where you live and reside. It's what gives you vision and the ability to face the world. If you don't have peace and blessing on that dwelling, you will have trouble.

DEDICATING YOUR HOUSE

14

DEDICATING YOUR HOUSE
STEP SEVEN

Take Communion When You Dedicate It

Jesus said to take communion as often as you want in order to remember Him.

> The Lord Jesus the same night in which he was betrayed took bread: And when he had given thanks, he brake it, and said, Take, eat: this is my body, which is broken for you: this do in remembrance of me. After the same manner also he took the cup, when he had supped, saying, this cup is the new testament in my blood: this do ye,

DEDICATING YOUR HOUSE

> as oft as ye drink it, in remembrance of me. For as often as ye eat this bread, and drink this cup, ye do shew the Lord's death till he come (1 Corinthians 11:23-26).

You can take communion to bring remembrance of Him into the house.

> Now the first day of the feast of unleavened bread the disciples came to Jesus, saying unto him, Where wilt thou that we prepare for thee to eat the passover? (Matthew 26:17).

This event took place just before Jesus went to Calvary. This is the time and the recognition of the Passover, and it's what Christians now refer to as our communion or the Lord's Supper.

In other words, the disciples are asking in this verse: where do you want us to go? What's the right place for us to do this religious thing—the church, the synagogue, or the temple?

Dedicating Your House—Step Seven

> And he said, Go into the city to such a man, and say unto him, The Master saith, My time is at hand; I will keep the passover at thy house with my disciples (Matthew 26:18).

There is absolutely nothing wrong with receiving communion in a house as long as the house is worthy. Jesus didn't go just anywhere; He went to a specific place of His choosing. The room where they took communion was the same place that 120 followers of Jesus would be later filled with the Holy Ghost on the day of Pentecost—the Upper Room. That was definitely a worthy house—a very worthy room in a very worthy house.

When you dedicate a house, make a point to receive communion there. You have a biblical example right here of sanctifying a place through communion.

DEDICATING YOUR HOUSE

15

DEDICATING YOUR HOUSE
STEP EIGHT

Give God an Offering

The biblical precedent for giving God an offering in the process of dedicating a house is found in Leviticus:

> "And he shall take to cleanse the house two birds, and cedar wood, and scarlet, and hyssop:" (Leviticus 14:49).

The blood cleanses the house. It goes without saying that the offering mentioned in Leviticus was an offering for that time, not ours. In today's world, we do not give offerings of birds, cedar wood, or scarlet and hyssop. Regardless, if you are going to dedicate your house to the Lord, you should bring Him an offering. It is important to receive communion and bring an offering to solidify the process. Those two actions will seal your covenant with God. You need to seal this covenant with an offering.

An Appropriate Offering

Just what is an appropriate offering? Unfortunately, I can't tell you. Although I can't expound on what an appropriate offering might be for you, I can give you some broad stroke examples of what I believe would be appropriate. These are a few examples of ways to bring an offering to the Lord that would be in good taste and performed with the dignity that would bring glory to the Lord. Although it is always an acceptable idea, I am not saying you have to bring your offering to your church. It wouldn't hurt, but you don't have to do that.

Dedicating Your House—Step Eight

Offering Ideas

- You may know of a young couple that loves the Lord who is trying to buy their first house. You could help them make the down payment.

- You may know someone who is struggling financially. You could make one or two house payments for them.

- You may want to give an offering to the house of the Lord in an amount equal to your house payment as a seed for your home's cleansing.

- You may want to give a special heirloom that you've had in your home for years—something that means a great deal to you—to someone who will truly appreciate it. It should not be some ugly, worthless piece of junk that you don't care anything about. Giving something that is just taking up space in a spare bedroom that you were going to throw away anyway isn't at all what I'm talking about. The important thing is to give from the heart, but never to someone who doesn't understand what you're doing.

What's a Reasonable Amount?

The question remains, "How much is too much, and how much is too little?" An excellent rule of thumb is realizing that Jesus is moved with the feelings of your infirmities, and if your offering touches you, it will touch Him, as well—no set amount required. It is a free-will offering, which means there are not any hard and fast rules, numbers, or percentages like there are with the tithe. This offering is done as you choose and in the way that you deem important. But, when you do it, you must do it in faith believing God to intervene in the process as you dedicate your house to the Lord.

Dedicating Your House—Step Eight

Don't Delay ... Dedicate!

Don't let this information and concepts get too far down the road. It's never too late to dedicate your home. Read and re-read this book until the truths from the Scripture concerning the dedication process become clear to you. However, far more important than just reading this book repeatedly, is actually taking the concepts and truths that you've learned, internalizing them, putting them into practice, and actually dedicating your house to the Lord.

Dedicate your house, and do it soon! You will be blessed that you did.

DEDICATING YOUR HOUSE

EIGHT WAYS TO PROPERLY DEDICATE YOUR HOUSE TO THE LORD

1. Set your house apart verbally for the Lord.

2. Cleanse your house from all uncleanness.

3. Walk your property lines.

4. Speak peace to the house.

5. Invite God's presence through prayer.

6. Speak blessings over your house and your property.

7. Take communion when you dedicate it.

8. Give God an offering.

ABOUT THE AUTHOR

DR. ED KING is the founder and Senior Pastor of Redemption Church in Knoxville, Tennessee. He is also the president of *The Power of the Word* television ministry which broadcasts to both national and international markets. He makes his home in Knoxville with his wife and co-pastor, Nora King. His daughter Laren also lives in Knoxville.

DEDICATING YOUR HOUSE

In addition to his responsibilities as the pastor of Redemption Church and his lead role at *Power of the Word*, Pastor King travels extensively and has ministered in over sixty nations around the world, teaching and preaching the gospel to thousands of people in leadership conferences and evangelistic meetings. Dr. King has authored of several books which include: ***Will My Pet Be in Heaven?, Loyalty: Going Beyond Faithfulness, The Timing of God: His Timetable for Your Life,*** and ***Dedicating Your House.***

REDEMPTION church

3550 Pleasant Ridge Road

Knoxville, TN 37921

865.521.7777

www.redemptionchurch.com

RedemptionChurchTN   RedemptionChurchTN   RedemptionTN

ed king
power of the word ministries

PO Box 52466

Knoxville, TN 37950

1.800.956.4433

www.poweroftheword.com

powbroadcast   powbroadcast

DEDICATING YOUR HOUSE
by Dr. Ed King

Dedicating your house is a rite that every Christian should perform in order to live a quiet and peaceful life. Because you live in your house, you should want and expect God's blessings on it. One way to see those blessings is to thoughtfully and sacredly separate your house for the Lord's work and service. In this book, Dr. King lays out the biblical case for dedicating your house and provides eight easy-to-follow steps.
ISBN: 9781602730861 • 114 pages.

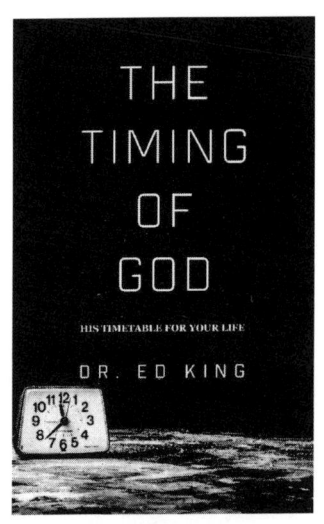

THE TIMING OF GOD—His Timetable for Your Life
by Dr. Ed King

In this life–changing book, you can begin your pursuit of the flawless timing of God by discovering the true timetable that God has set up for you at creation. You will see everything in life has a time and a season. God wants to give you remarkable things to experience, but He wants to give them to you when you are ready to handle and enjoy them. After reading and studying this book, you will become more assured than ever that your next move will be by the inspiration and the timing of God.

ISBN: 978160273717 • 118 pages.

LOYALTY: GOING BEYOND FAITHFULNESS
by Dr. Ed King

Pastor Ed King elaborates on the distinctions between faithfulness and loyalty and focuses on lessons learned by looking at the brotherly love of Jonathan and David. Learn how God's grace will meet you to go past faithfulness and enter into loyalty. It all starts with a decision!
ISBN: 9781602730793 • 110 pages.

WILL MY PET BE IN HEAVEN?
by Dr. Ed King

In this book, Pastor Ed King gives us a solid, biblical answer about your pet's afterlife. If you or someone you know has lost a pet, you will find great comfort and insight into what the Bible has to say about our beloved animals and their future in heaven.
ISBN: 9781602730687 • 92 pages

10 Major Life Lessons—CD series
This series will upgrade your life in every way. You'll learn the power of a seed, the importance of forgiveness, how to live a disciplined life, and much more. Apply these ten lessons, and you'll go further than you ever thought possible.

Conquering Life's Limitations—CD series
As Christians, we have the mind of Christ with no limitations on what God can reveal to you if we're open to it. Listen as Pastor Nora King explains how wisdom is the most important thing if we want to conquer life's limitations.

Divine Healing & the Atonement—CD series
Are you aware of the healing power that is available to you? In Pastor King's message, you can discover the meaning of Jesus' atonement and how He satisfied the judgement against us to bring us righteousness and healing

Faith: How May It Help You?—CD series
God never intended for His family to live a life of lack, struggle or defeat. We can take the gift of faith, and by activating it, we can create an exciting and victorious life.

Grace vs. Works—CD series
For by grace we are saved through faith—it is a gift of God, not of works. Grace verses works—they both have to be looked at; they have to be thought about; and they have to be considered. Both are biblical truths and are important to believers.

Heaven—CD series
We hear a lot about Heaven. What does the Bible say about it? This 11-part series establishes a foundational truth on our future home. Heaven is a real place; a place to look forward to. Insightful teachings like these are a must for every believer.

How to Study the Bible—CD series
In this series, you'll learn some of the personal study habits and recommended study tools of a man with 30 years of experience in learning the Bible and a ministry for teaching.

Keeping Hope Alive—CD series
In this series, the importance of keeping hope alive is revealed, along with ways we misplace our hope and how to break through the bondage of despair. Hope is a vital part of who you are in Christ.

Truth: Your Baseline for Life—CD series
Through this 5-CD series by Pastor Ed King, you will discover how truth relates to your freedom, relationships, character, wisdom, and more. You can begin today to live a life of power and liberty.

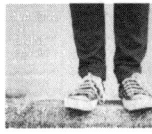

Walking in Divine Favor—CD series
In this CD series, Pastor Ed King teaches keys to living in favor with God and man. Learn the importance of honor and integrity in relationships, cheerful giving, grateful receiving, and more. The keys listed in this insightful series will move you forward faster than you can move yourself alone.

Parsons Publishing House
Your Voice Your World™

30 DAYS TO A BETTER PRAYER LIFE
by Pastor Nora King

In this exciting book, Nora King offers fresh revelation and practical teaching to help you experience the release of God's power. You will learn daily how to improve your prayer life and enter God's presence through these simple principles. You don't have to struggle in prayer any longer!
ISBN: 9781602730120 • 142 pages.

Available at your local bookstore or order online at www.Amazon.com

Parsons Publishing House
Your Voice Your World™

NEXT LEVEL
Raising the Standard of Grace
by Pastor Robert Gay
ISBN: 9781602730427 • 216 pages • $14.95 USD.

CAPTURING THE HEART OF GOD
Pleasing the Father in Everyday Life
by Diane Parsons
ISBN: 9781602080082 • 128 pages • $10.95 USD.

OUT OF BALANCE INTO RHYTHM
Finding Joy and Peace as You Live Life with God
by Frank Maycock
ISBN: 9781602730786 • 192 pages • $14.95 USD.

SETTING THE COURSE FOR FUTURE GENERATIONS
by Shane Huseby
ISBN: 9781602730243 • 120 pages • $9.95 USD.

SURVIVING THE CHALLENGES OF TRANSITION
by Dr. Gerald Doggett
ISBN: 9781602730182 • 140 pages • $12.95 USD.

Parsons Publishing House
Your Voice Your World™

EMERGING AS AN INNOVATIVE CHRISTIAN LEADER
by Dr. Darrell Parsons
ISBN: 9781602730656 • 228 pages • $14.95 USD.

JESUS IN 3D
Living in the Fullness of God
by Pastor Robert Gay
ISBN: 9781602730588 • 102 pages • $9.95 USD.

BUILDING STRONG
God's Blueprint for Building the Church
by Pastor Robert Gay
ISBN: 9781602730892 • 224 pages • $14.95 USD.

SILENCING THE ENEMY WITH PRAISE
by Pastor Robert Gay
ISBN: 9781602730052 • 156 pages • $11.95 USD.

SONSHIP
The Mantle. The Journey. The Double Portion.
by Pastor Joshua Gay
ISBN: 9781602730526 • 180 pages • $12.95 USD.

Parsons Publishing House
Your Voice Your World™

70 REASONS FOR SPEAKING IN TONGUES
Your Own Built in Spiritual Dynamo
by Dr. Bill Hamon
ISBN: 9781602730137 • 216 pages • $14.95 USD.

UPRIGHTING RELATIONSHIPS
by Linda Roeder
ISBN: 9781602730755 • 174 pages • $12.95 USD.

FAITH AFTER FAILURE
Reconnecting with Your Destiny
by Sandie Freed
ISBN: 9781602730557 • 208 pages • $13.95 USD.

WHY DO I DO THE THINGS I DO?
Understanding Personalities
by Dr. Darrell Parsons
ISBN: 9781602730199 • 132 pages • $10.95 USD.

RELEASE YOUR WORDS—IMPACT YOUR WORLD
by Dr. Darrell Parsons
ISBN: 9781602730007 • 140 pages • $9.95 USD.